Ed Parman
Box 215
Osceo, Mo.

GW01513946

WHERE DO I GO FROM HERE, GOD?

WHERE DO I GO FROM HERE, GOD?

Zac Poonen

TYNDALE HOUSE PUBLISHERS
Wheaton, Illinois

Coverdale House Publishers Ltd.
London, England

Library of Congress Catalog Card Number 70-188536
ISBN 8423-8200-3

Copyright © 1971 by Gospel Literature Service, under the title *Finding God's Will*. This Tyndale House edition published by permission of Gospel Literature Service.

Second printing, December 1972

Printed in the United States of America.

CONTENTS

PREFACE: THIS BOOK – AND YOU / 7

1 A PLAN FOR YOUR LIFE / 11

2 CONDITIONS FOR FINDING GOD'S WILL / 21

3 GUIDANCE THROUGH THE INNER WITNESS / 43

4 GUIDANCE THROUGH EXTERNAL MEANS / 52

5 VOCATIONAL CALLING / 70

6 FINAL CONSIDERATIONS / 77

THIS BOOK – AND YOU

Many young believers today are eager to know how to find the will of God. This book is an attempt to help them. It presents no perfect formula for infallible guidance, for the Bible presents none. We must beware of seeking divine guidance in a mechanical rather than in a spiritual way.

This book is not meant to provide you with all the answers. Its main purpose is to encourage you to be more dependent on the Holy Spirit. Watchman Nee has said, "We human beings are not to produce 'perfect' books. The danger of such perfection is that a man can understand without the help of the Holy Spirit. But if God gives us books they will ever be broken fragments, not always clear or consistent or logical, lacking conclusions, and yet coming to us in life and ministering life to us. We cannot dissect divine facts and outline and systematize them. It is only the immature Christian who demands always to have intellectually satisfying conclusions. The Word of God itself has this fundamental character, that it speaks always and essentially to our spirit and to our life." May this book impart not merely information to your mind, but above all, life to your spirit.

I have not used the King James Version lest its archaic language prevent us from understanding the real meaning of Scripture. I have instead used modern translations for all Scripture quotations. I once heard an adaptation of the incident described in Acts 8:30, 31. Philip asks the Ethiopian statesman, "Do you understand what you are reading?" The latter replies, "How can I unless some one gives me a modern translation?"

Scripture quotations are from the Amplified Bible[1] except where otherwise stated. Phillips refers to J. B. Phillip's translation of the New Testament.[2] TLB refers to Kenneth Taylor's paraphrase of the Scriptures.[3] NASB refers to the New American Standard Bible.[4] I gratefully acknowledge permission to use the quotations from these versions.

I am indebted to a number of the Lord's servants who read through the original manuscript of this book and offered helpful suggestions.

Zac Poonen

---

[1] *The Amplified Old Testament* © Zondervan Publishing House.

The Amplified New Testament © Lockman Foundation.
[2]J. B. Phillips' *New Testament in Modern Speech*
© Geoffrey Bles Ltd. Publishers
[3]*The Living Bible* © Tyndale House Publishers.
[4]*New American Standard Bible* © Lockman Foundation.

CHAPTER ONE

A PLAN FOR YOUR LIFE

Man's greatest honor and privilege is to do the will of God. This was what the Lord Jesus taught his disciples. He once said that only those who did his Father's will would enter the kingdom of heaven (Matthew 7:21). He also said that his true brothers and sisters were those who did the will of God (Matthew 12:50).

This emphasis was duly passed on by the apostles to their generation. Peter declared that God sets men free from sin so that they can do his will (1 Peter 4:1, 2). Paul asserted that believers are created anew in Christ Jesus so that they can walk in a path God has already mapped out for them. He therefore exhorted the Ephesian Christians not to be foolish, but to understand what the will of the Lord was for their lives (Ephesians 2:10; 5:17). He prayed for the Colossian Christians that they might be filled with the knowledge of God's will. He told them that his coworker Epaphras was also praying for them that they might fulfill all the will of God (Colossians 1:9; 4:12). The apostle John taught that only those who did the will of God would abide forever (1 John 2:17).

This emphasis is unfortunately rare in our day and generation. Hence the shallowness and powerlessness of the average believer today. Men are urged to come to Jesus merely to receive forgiveness. In apostolic times, people were told that forgiveness of sins was to be only a prelude to a life dedicated to the fulfilment of the whole will of God.

Acts 13:22 seems to imply that David was called "a man after God's own heart" because he desired to do the will of God alone. David himself tells us elsewhere that he delighted in doing God's will (Psalm 40:8). He was not a perfect man. He committed many sins, some very serious ones, for which God had to punish him severely. Yet God forgave him and found pleasure in him because basically David wanted to do all of God's will. This encourages us to believe that in spite of all our imperfections, we too can be men and women after God's own heart — if only our hearts are set on doing his will.

The New Testament urges believers to walk as Jesus walked, following his example. The guiding principle of Jesus' entire life and ministry was to do the will of his Father. He never moved until his Father told him to. And when he did move, neither the threats of his enemies nor the pleadings of his friends could stop him from doing what his Father required of him. His daily food was to do his Father's will (John 4: 34). As men crave for food to nourish their bodies, he craved to do the will of the one who had sent him.

Every believer should have a similar hunger to fulfill all the will of God. How easy it is to pray, "Thy will be done on earth as it is in Heaven," and then to do just as we please, without seeking God's guidance in our daily lives.

GOD'S PLAN IS THE BEST

It is the height of folly not to seek God's guidance. If you were alone in the middle of a thick forest on a pitch dark night, not knowing which way to turn, you would be glad to have with you someone who knew every inch of the forest and whom you could trust fully. You would soon follow without question whatever way he took. It would be foolish to ignore his advice, to move on your own into that dark and dense forest, full of hidden dangers. Yet many believers do just that sort of thing.

The future that lies before us is darker than anything on earth could possibly be. We can see nothing ahead. Yet we have to move forward.

We often come to crossroads in our lives,

where we have to make decisions with far-reaching consequences. Decisions such as the choice of a career and of a life partner affect our entire future. How are we to decide at such times? We know nothing of the dangers and the hidden pitfalls along each path. We know nothing of the snares Satan has laid for us. And yet — we have to decide which path to take.

It would therefore be not only desirable but necessary for us to have someone beside us at such times whom we can trust fully, who knows the entire future. We have just such a person in the Lord Jesus Christ, and he is more than eager to guide us along the safest and best path.

The Bible teaches that God has a specific plan for each of our lives (Ephesians 2:10). He has planned a career for us, chosen a life partner for us, and even planned where we should live and what we should do each day. In every case, his choice must be the best, for he knows us so well and he takes every factor into consideration. It is wise then to seek his will in all matters — major as well as minor.

It is not only foolish but dangerous to follow the reasonings of our limited intellects and the dictates of our emotions alone. Unless we are gripped by the conviction that God's plan is indeed the best, we are not likely to be in earnest about seeking it.

Many have made shipwreck of their lives by failing to seek the will of God right from their youth. It is indeed "good for a man that he bear the yoke in his youth" (Lamentations 3:27). In Matthew 11:28-30, Jesus invites us to take his yoke upon us. What does it mean to take the yoke? In the villages of India, the farmers plow their fields with pairs of oxen. The oxen are kept together by a yoke upon their necks. When a new ox is to be trained to plow, it is yoked together with an experienced ox. The new one is thus compelled to walk in the *same direction* and at the *same speed* as the older ox.

This is what it means to take the yoke of Jesus upon us. We shall have to walk with Jesus in the path that pleases him, never rushing ahead to do anything without his leading, nor lagging behind when he calls to some new step of obedience. Few understand this meaning of the yoke. Fewer still are willing to accept it. The ox is forced by its owner to take the yoke upon its neck. But Jesus *invites* us. There is no compulsion here. How foolish we are to reject this invitation! We would rather take the heavy yoke of our own self-will with its accompanying frustrations, defeats, and regrets, than the light yoke of Jesus that brings true liberty and deep rest!

"Come to me and I will give you rest — all of you who work so hard beneath a heavy yoke. Wear my yoke . . . and let me teach you [as the older ox teaches the inexperienced one] . . . and you shall find rest for your souls; for I give you only light burdens" (Matthew 11:28-30 — TLB).

We read of Enoch that he "walked with God" (Genesis 5:22) — i.e., he did not rush ahead nor lag behind, but walked in God's appointed path as one under the yoke — for three hundred years. As a result, God testified that he was pleased with Enoch's life (Hebrews 11:5). This is the only way that we can please God — by living and moving under his yoke, in his perfect will. Only thus shall we be able to stand before him without regret when he comes again.

MISSING GOD'S PLAN

It is possible for a believer to miss God's perfect will for his life. Saul was chosen by God to be king over Israel, but eventually, as a result of his impatience and disobedience, God had to reject him. (See 1 Samuel 13 and 15.) True, he remained on the throne for some years more, but he had missed God's will for his life. Solomon is another example. He pleased God in his earlier years, but fell away later through marrying heathen women.

Twice in the New Testament we are exhorted to take a warning from the example of the Israelites who perished in the wilderness. God's perfect will for them was that they should enter Canaan. But all except two of them missed God's best through unbelief and disobedience (1 Corinthians 10:1-12; Hebrews 3:7-14). Many believers have similarly missed God's perfect plan for their lives through disobedience and compromise — often in marriage or in the choice of a career.

G. Christian Weiss in his book, *The Perfect Will of God*, tells of a teacher in a Bible school who told his students one day, "I have lived most of my life on God's second best." God had called him to be a missionary in his younger days, but he had turned aside from that calling as a result of marriage. He then began a selfish business life, working in a bank, with the primary purpose of making money. God continued to speak to him for a number of years, but he refused to yield. One day his little child had a fall from a chair and died. This drove him to his knees, and after a whole night spent in tears before God, he put his life into God's hands completely. It was too late for him to go to Africa; that door was closed. He knew that had been God's best for him, but he had missed it. All that he could do was to ask God to put the rest of his life to some use. He became a teacher in a Bible school, but could never forget that this was only God's second best.

Weiss continues, "I have since met numerous people who have borne similar testimony. Usually these testimonies have been bathed, or at least marked, with bitter tears. For while, thank God, He has ways of using even those who have sinned and have gone past that single entrance into the channel of His perfect will, *life can never be the way He originally intended it*. It is a tragedy to miss the perfect will of God for one's life. Christian, mark well these words and this testimony lest you too miss His first choice. God, doubtless, will use any life that is submitted to His Hands, anywhere along life's pathway, but let us be among those who have sought and surrendered to His will at the outset of life's journey, and thus avoid those painful and shameful detours along the way."

We just cannot live the victorious life, or be of maximum use to the Lord, or be a blessing to others in any place we choose. Some may feel that they can choose their own career and their place of residence and then seek to be a witness for the Lord wherever they are. The Lord may in his mercy use such believers in a limited way. But their usefulness in God's vineyard will be only a fraction of what it could have been had they earnestly sought his plan and remained in the center of his perfect will. Stunted spiritual growth and limited fruitfulness are the consequences of a careless disregard of God's laws.

If you have disobeyed God in some matter, turn to him in repentance *now*, before it is too late. It may yet be possible for you, as in Jonah's case, to come back into the mainstream of God's plan for your life.

Each of us has but one life. Blessed is the man who, like Paul, can say at the end of it that he has finished his God-appointed task (2 Timothy 4:7).

"The world and all its passionate desires will one day disappear. But the man who is following God's will is part of the permanent and cannot die" (1 John 2:17 — Phillips).

"Live life, then, with a due sense of responsibility, not as men who do not know the meaning and purpose of life but as *those who do.* Make the best use of your time, despite all the difficulties of these days. Don't be vague but firmly grasp what you know to be the will of the Lord" (Ephesians 5:15-17 — Phillips).

When I stand at the judgment seat of Christ,
  And He shows me His plan for me,
The plan of my life as it might have been
  Had He had His way, and I see

How I blocked Him here, and I checked Him there,
  And I would not yield my will; —
Will there be grief in my Saviour's eyes,
  Grief though He loves me still?

He would have me rich, and I stand there poor,
  Stripped of all but His grace,
While memory runs like a hunted thing
  Down the paths I cannot retrace.

Then my desolate heart will well-nigh break
  With the tears I cannot shed;
I shall cover my face with my empty hands,
  I shall bow my uncrowned head.

Lord of the years that are left to me,
  I give them to Thy hand;
Take me, and break me, and mould me
  To the pattern Thou hast planned.
              — *Martha Snell Nicholson*

SUMMARY

1. The Lord Jesus and his apostles taught that man's greatest honor and privilege is to do the will of God.
2. It is foolish to move into the future on our own when God is waiting to guide us. His plan is the best. If we yield to him, he can save us from Satan's snares.
3. It is possible to miss God's perfect will for our lives through carelessness or disobedience.

CHAPTER TWO

CONDITIONS FOR FINDING GOD'S WILL

Divine guidance cannot be considered apart from our personal relationship with God. Many desire the gifts but not the Giver. If we long for guidance but do not thirst for God himself, we shall not obtain the guidance we seek.

A person must be in fellowship with God in order to experience his guidance in his life. This implies, first of all, that he should have a vital relationship with Christ through the new birth. But this alone is not enough. There are certain other essential conditions to be fulfilled if we are to know God's leading. These prerequisites are mentioned in two passages of Scripture, one in the Old Testament and the other in the New (Proverbs 3:5, 6; Romans 12:1, 2). Let us consider these passages in detail.

FAITH

> *"Trust in the Lord with all your heart and mind . . . and He will direct your paths"* (Proverbs 3:5, 6).

There are many who never come to a knowledge of God's will, because they simply do not believe God will guide them. Faith is a prime prerequisite when we are seeking God's guidance. By faith we mean not merely a mental acceptance of truth but a confidence in God that comes through personal knowledge of him.

When we lack wisdom (knowledge of God's mind in a certain situation) we are invited to ask God for this and we are promised that he will grant it to us in abundance — provided we ask in faith. The one who asks without faith invariably receives nothing (James 1:5-7).

Young believers may feel divine guidance is available only to mature Christians who have grown in the knowledge of the Lord for several years. It is no doubt true that the more we walk with God, the better we can discern his mind. Nevertheless it is also true that God desires to guide all his children. What was said to Paul is true for all of us — "God . . . has destined *and* appointed you to come progressively to know His will — that is, to perceive, to recognize more strongly and clearly and to become better and more intimately acquainted with His will" (Acts 22:14).

A father gladly reveals to his children his desires and plans for them — not only to the older ones but to the younger ones as well. It is the same with our heavenly Father. God has said in his Word that in this day of the New Covenant (or Testament) *all* his children — "from the smallest to the greatest" — will know him personally (Hebrews 8:10, 11). Every one of us then can come to him "with the full assurance of faith" that he delights to make his will known to his seeking children.

In Hebrews 11:6, we are told that without faith it is impossible to please God. The verse goes on to say that those who come to God must believe that he is a rewarder of those who earnestly and diligently seek him. The evidence of a person's faith is found in his *persistence in prayer*. The one who doubts will stop praying very soon. But the one who believes will lay hold of God *until* he gets an answer. God honors earnestness because it is the product of a strong faith. We cannot receive anything precious from God without intensely desiring it first. "He satisfies [only] the longing soul" (Psalm 107:9). God has said, "Then you will seek Me, inquire for and require Me as a vital necessity and find Me; when you search for Me with all your heart" (Jeremiah 29:13).

Is it not true that when seeking God's guidance we have often gone about it halfheartedly? When Jesus sought the Father's will in the garden of Gethsemane, he prayed again and again "in desperate prayer and the agony of tears"

(Hebrews 5:7 — Phillips). How casual our seeking is when compared to that. We often seek God's will with no more earnestness than we would have when searching for a lost dime! No wonder we don't find it. If we value the will of God as the greatest treasure on earth, we will seek it with all our hearts.

Do we really believe that God rewards diligent seekers? Then our faith will manifest itself in incessant prayer. If we are consumed with earnest desire to fulfill his will in every area of our lives, God will undoubtedly reveal his mind to us. He will certainly honor a faith that lays hold of him until it receives an answer.

In the Bible faith is often coupled with *patience*. Both are necessary if we are to inherit God's promises (Hebrews 6:12, 15). David exhorts us (no doubt from his own experience) to commit our way to the Lord, trusting in him and waiting patiently for his time. We are assured that he will not let us down (Psalm 37:5, 7). One of the greatest temptations when seeking God's guidance is to fret and become impatient. But the believing heart is a restful one.

There are some decisions for which we don't need to wait for a perfectly clear indication of the mind of the Lord. For example, if you are seeking the Lord's will as to whether you should commence a journey on the 15th or the 16th of the month, you need not wait indefinitely for a clear word from him.

Yet there are some decisions for which we

must wait until we are perfectly clear about the will of God. When considering marriage, for example, we cannot afford to be uncertain. We have to be perfectly sure of God's will before deciding. Such a decision is obviously of greater moment than the former one, because its effects are more far-reaching. The more important the decision, the longer we may have to wait to be sure of God's will.

If we trust in the Lord, we won't be afraid to wait. We will not seek to grab for ourselves ahead of God's time, out of fear that we might lose the best by waiting. God is well able to safeguard the best for us in every realm. When we grab impatiently, we invariably miss the Lord's best. The Bible says that "he who believes . . . will not make haste" (Isaiah 28:16).

In Psalm 25, the great "Guidance" psalm, David speaks again and again of waiting on the Lord (vv. 3, 5, 21). None who waits for the Lord's time will ever regret having waited, for God "works and shows Himself active on behalf of him who [earnestly] waits for Him" (Isaiah 64:4; cf. 49:23).

Often, it is only as we wait that God can make his mind clear to us. James McConkey in his booklet, *Guidance*, has written, "Sometimes you draw from the tap a glass of water which is muddy and turbid. How do you clear it? You place the glass of muddy water on your table. Moment by moment the sediment deposits at the bottom of the glass. Gradually the water grows clearer. In a few moments it is so clear that you may distinguish objects through it. It has all been brought about simply by waiting. The law is the same in the realm of guidance. Here too, God's great precipitant is waiting. . . . As we do so, the sediment slowly settles. . . . The trifling things assume their proper subordinate place. The big things loom up into their proper importance. Waiting is the solution of it all. . . . The vast majority of our mistakes come from neglect of it. Haste is more often a trap of Satan than it is a necessity of guidance . . .

"Sometimes our perplexity is so great that it seems no guidance will ever come. For such times the psalmist has a precious message in his word about the night-watchers. 'I am looking and waiting for the Lord more than watchmen for the morning' (Psalm 130:6). How do men, who wait in the night hours for the dawn, watch for the morning? The answer is fourfold: —

> They watch in *darkness*.
> They watch for that which *comes slowly*.
> They watch for that which is *sure to come*.
> They watch for that which when it does come *brings the light of day*.

"So it is with us who wait for guidance. Often our perplexity is so extreme that we seem to be waiting in *total darkness*. Often too as we wait, even as those who wait for the day, the first faint streaks of dawn seem to come, oh, *so slowly!* Then too, as there never yet has been a night which was not sure to end in the dawn, so our night of uncertainty is sure to end in the dawning light of God's guidance. Lastly, as the slow-coming dawn, when it does arrive, brings light and blessing without measure, so when our God-given guidance at last breaks upon us it will so gladden our waiting souls and so *illumine* our beclouded path, we shall almost forget the long days when we waited in darkness."

Beware of being in a hurry. Impatience always stems from unbelief. It was said of the Israelites in the wilderness that "they did not [earnestly] wait for His plans [to develop] respecting them" (Psalm 106:13). They missed God's best thereby. May God save us from such a tragedy.

SELF-DISTRUST

> *"Do not rely on your own insight or understanding. . . . and He will direct your paths"* (Proverbs 3:5, 6).

The one who does not distrust his own natural wisdom in spiritual matters has yet to learn one of the fundamental lessons of the Christian life. Meager intelligence cannot by itself deprive a man of the knowledge of God's will, if the man leans upon God. But proud dependence on one's own cleverness and foresight can. Paul says in Philippians 3:3 that a believer should be characterized by a lack of confidence in himself.

Paul was a mighty intellectual, but he still had to distrust himself and lean upon God. From his own experience he writes to the Corinthian Christians, "If any man among you thinks himself one of the world's clever ones, let him discard his cleverness that he may learn to be truly wise. For this world's cleverness is stupidity to God" (1 Corinthians 3:18, 19 – Phillips). Worldly wisdom is a hindrance to the knowing of God's will, and so must be discarded.

Lest this last statement be misunderstood, let me add a word of explanation. Rejecting worldly wisdom does not mean the nonuse of our intellectual abilities. Paul used his and it is unthinkable that he would ever ask others not to use theirs. Worldly wisdom cannot refer to education and learning, for both the learned Paul and the unlearned Corinthians (to whom he was writing) had to discard it. It refers to the measure of trust we put in our own cleverness, whether our learning be much or little. It is a malady that can afflict the learned and the unlearned alike.

The Bible likens believers to sheep. A sheep is a foolish animal, unable to find its own way around, and extremely shortsighted. Its only safety lies in following its shepherd wherever he goes. This is a very humiliating fact for self-confident man to acknowledge. His pride will rebel at the very suggestion of his being stupid in spiritual matters. Yet this utter distrust of self is an inescapable preliminary to knowing God's guidance in our lives. David took the place of a sheep before the Lord and thereby experienced divine guidance — "The Lord is my Shepherd . . . He leads me . . . He leads me" (Psalm 23: 1-3).

Unless man humbles himself and takes this lowly place, he cannot know the ways of God. "He will teach the ways that are right and best to those who humbly turn to him," said David in Psalm 25:9 (TLB). Self-confidence may be all right for the man of the world but certainly not for the child of God. Herein lies the reason why many believers miss God's plan for their lives. Confident of their own abilities, they do not earnestly seek the will of God. They depend instead upon their own genius and are thus led astray.

God often allows failure and confusion in our lives in order that we might see the total depravity of our hearts and the unreliability of our fallible intellects, and thus learn the necessity of clinging more closely to him. One of the chief lessons which the Lord sought to teach his disciples was that without him they could do nothing (John 15:5). They were very slow in learning this, and so are we.

The humble man who recognizes his limitations and leans heavily upon God will ascertain the divine will without difficulty. The self-confident doctor of theology, on the other hand, who depends on his seminary training, will be left groping in the darkness.

OBEDIENCE IN EVERY AREA

"In all your ways acknowledge Him, and He will direct your paths" (Proverbs 3:6).

We are sometimes eager to know God's guidance in one area of our lives, but not so keen on having his direction in other areas. For example, we may earnestly seek God's will in marriage, but may not do so when looking for a job. Or it could be vice versa. Or perhaps we may seek God's guidance as to how and where to spend our annual vacation, but may never ask him how to spend our money.

This is because we are inclined to want God's guidance only when it is convenient for us. It takes a long time before selfish motives are totally purged from our hearts. We seek God's will in some matters because we don't want to make mistakes that might cause us suffering or loss. The motive is not that we might please God but that we might be comfortable and prosperous. Hence we fail to receive God's guidance, for he has promised to guide only those who acknowledge him in *all* their ways, those who gladly accept his direction in every area of their lives.

There are many areas in which God's will is already revealed to us in the Scriptures. For instance, the Bible says that God wants us to be holy and thankful: *"This is the will of God,* that you should be consecrated — separated and set apart for pure and holy living. . . ."; "Thank [God] in everything — no matter what the circumstances may be, be thankful and give thanks; for *this is the will of God* for you [who are] in Christ Jesus" (1 Thessalonians 4:3; 5:18).

Similarly, we are told that God expects us to love our neighbors as ourselves (Romans 13:9). If we have received God's forgiveness and salvation, we should desire the same for our neighbors. God's will is clearly revealed in the New Testament: we are to be his witnesses (Acts 1:8).

Loving our neighbors implies a concern primarily for their spiritual needs, but does not exclude their other needs. God has said, "I want you to share your food with the hungry and bring right into your own homes those who are helpless, poor and destitute. Clothe those who are cold and don't hide from relatives who need your help. If you do these things, *God will shed his own glorious light upon you.* . . . Then, when you call, the Lord will answer. 'Yes, I am here,' he will quickly reply. All you need to do is to stop oppressing the weak, and to stop making false accusations and spreading vicious rumors! Feed the hungry! Help those in trouble! Then your light will shine out from the darkness, and the darkness around you shall be as bright as day. *And the Lord will guide you continually*" (Isaiah 58:7-11 — TLB). God delights to reveal his mind to those who are unselfishly concerned with the needs of others.

If we fail to obey the Lord in these areas where he has already revealed his will, then we cannot expect him to guide us in other spheres. It is a principle of divine guidance that God never grants further light to one who ignores the light he already has. God will not show us the second step before we take the first. "As you go, *step by step,* I will open up the way before you," is his promise (Proverbs 4:12 — paraphrase). He is interested in our every step. "The steps of a [good] man are directed and established of the Lord, when He delights in his way [and He busies Himself with his every step]" (Psalm 37:23).

Here is another promise of guidance for the obedient: "I will instruct you (says the Lord) and guide you along the best pathway for your life; I will advise you and watch your progress, [but] don't be like a senseless horse or mule" (Psalm 32:8, 9 — TLB). (The horse is characterized by impatience, always wanting to rush ahead, whereas the mule is characterized by stubbornness, often refusing to move forward. We must avoid both these attitudes.)

God speaks to us through our consciences when we are disobedient. We must be careful, then, to heed the voice of conscience always. Jesus said, "Your eye is the lamp of your body; when your eye . . . is sound and fulfilling its office, your whole body is full of light" (Luke 11:34). What did Jesus mean by the eye? In Matthew 5:8, he connected spiritual vision with purity of heart. So the eye must refer to the conscience which, when obeyed, constantly leads us to purity of heart.

By itself, conscience is not the voice of God, for it is educated and determined by the principles on which a person bases his life. But if it is obeyed constantly and brought in line with the teaching of the Bible, it will reflect God's standard increasingly. The promise in Luke 11:34, then, is that if we keep our conscience clean we shall have God's light flooding our lives — and thus we shall know his will. If we fail to listen to the voice of conscience in our daily lives, we shall fail to hear the voice of the Spirit when seeking God's guidance. Instant obedience to God whenever he speaks to us is one of the secrets of guidance.

Recently, I read of a fifteen-year-old boy, blind from birth, who flew and landed an aircraft safely. This remarkable feat was accomplished by his instantly obeying every order given by his instructor pilot. When facing life's manifold problems, we may feel like blind men trying to land a plane on an unknown and invisible runway. But if we develop the habit of instant obedience to God's commands, we shall find that we land safely.

UNCONDITIONAL YIELDEDNESS

"Make a decisive dedication of your bodies — presenting all your members and faculties — as a living sacrifice, holy and well pleasing to God. . . . so that you may prove [for your-

selves] what is the good and acceptable and perfect will of God" (Romans 12:1, 2).

The New Testament exhorts us to become bondslaves of the Lord. Paul called himself a willing bondslave of Jesus Christ. In the Old Testament there were two classes of servants — the bondslave and the hired servant. A bondslave, unlike the hired servant, was never paid. He was bought by his master for a price and as a result all that he was and all that he possessed belonged to his master. This is what every believer must recognize himself to be — a bondslave. Our time, money, talents, families, possessions, minds and bodies — all — belong to our Master and our Lord, for they are his by right of purchase on the cross (1 Corinthians 6:19, 20).

We are therefore exhorted to present our bodies to God, once for all, as a living sacrifice, even as the burnt offering in the Old Testament. The burnt offering, unlike the sin offering, was wholly offered to God and signified the offerer's utter dedication to him. When a man offered a burnt offering, he received nothing back. God could do whatever he liked with that offering. It was symbolic of Calvary's cross where the Lord Jesus offered himself utterly to his Father, saying, "Father, not my will but thine be done." This is what it means to present our body as a living sacrifice to God. We must die to our own will and choice as to how and where our body should be used by him. Only thus can we know his will.

Lack of such yieldedness is usually the main reason why we are unable to ascertain God's will. Our yieldedness to the Lord is often with reservations. We are not really willing to accept *anything* that God may offer.

I met a man once who was willing to take up any vocation except the Christian ministry. I told him that it was this reservation that kept him from being clear about God's plan for his life. When he finally yielded all to the Lord, he immediately gained a deeper assurance of God's will. God did not call him to the ministry, but he wanted him to be willing.

Many who come to God under the pretext of wanting to know his will really want only his approval of the path they have already chosen for themselves. Hence they receive no answer from him. How soon our problems of guidance would be solved, if only we gave ourselves without any reserve to our Lord saying, "Lord, I am willing to accept *anything*, if you will only assure me that it is your will. Choose for me, my Lord. I have no choice of my own in this matter." It was Abraham's willingness to go *anywhere* and to do *anything* at *anytime* for God that made him the "friend of God."

George Mueller of Bristol (England) was a man of great faith and one who could ascertain the will of God with remarkable accuracy. He has said in this connection, "I seek at the beginning to get my heart into such a state that it has no will of its own in regard to a given matter.

Nine-tenths of the trouble with people is just here. Nine-tenths of the difficulties are overcome when our hearts are ready to do the Lord's will, *whatever it may be.* When one is truly in this state, it is usually but a little way to the knowledge of what His will is."

Some want to know God's will first before deciding whether to obey or not. But God does not reveal his will to such people. Jesus said, "If any man desires to do His will . . . he will know . . ." (John 7:17). A willingness to do *anything* that God commands will alone qualify us to know what his perfect will is. This applies to small matters as well as big.

"Choose for us, God, nor let our weak preferring
Cheat us of good Thou hast for us designed;
Choose for us, God; Thy wisdom is unerring,
And we are fools and blind."

A RENEWED MIND

> *"Do not be conformed to this world . . . But be transformed by the [entire] renewal of your mind — by its new ideals and its new attitude — so that you may prove [for yourselves] what is the good and acceptable and perfect will of God"* (Romans 12:2).

Worldliness plugs our spirit's ears, preventing us from hearing God's voice. Every person living in this world is affected by its spirit. No one has escaped its influence. From childhood every one of us imbibes into himself, day by day, either more or less of the spirit of this world — by what we hear, see and read. This especially affects our minds and influences our thinking. The decisions we make then come primarily from worldly considerations.

The Spirit of God who comes to live in us when we are "born again" is opposed to the spirit of this world and therefore desires to renew our thinking completely. God's ultimate purpose for us is that we might be conformed to the image of his Son. This is the *primary* part of his will for all of us. Everything else — whom we should marry, where we should live and work — is secondary. All of God's dealings with us are directed towards this end — that we might become like Jesus (see Romans 8:28 and 29). But this can be fulfilled in us only as we allow the Holy Spirit to renew our minds daily. The more our minds are thus renewed the more accurately shall we be able to discern the will of God at life's crossroads.

Worldliness is not basically something external — such as attending movies, drinking, smoking, wearing expensive and fashionable clothes and jewelry, or living extravagantly. These may denote a worldly person, but they are only outward expressions of his worldly thought processes. Conformity to the world exists essentially in a person's mind and shows itself in various ways, especially in his decisions. For example, when considering a job or a career, a worldly person will be governed chiefly by factors such as salary, promotion prospects, comfort, ease, convenience, etc. And when contemplating marriage, he will be influenced by points such as family status, position in life, physical beauty, or wealth.

A believer's decisions, on the other hand, should be governed primarily by spiritual factors, although other considerations should not be neglected. The glory of God's name and the extension of his kingdom should be our first concern. This is why the Lord taught us first to pray, "Hallowed be thy name, thy kingdom come," and only then, "Thy will be done."

The process of discerning and eliminating worldly motives is vital if we are to know the will of God. To say, "God led me," when our motives were selfish, is blasphemy. Far better in such cases to say the decision was our own than to take God's name in vain and give a cloak of spirituality to our worldliness. We gain nothing by merely convincing others (or even ourselves) that we are doing God's will. After all, God cannot be fooled. As the Bible says, "We can always 'prove' that we are right, but is the Lord convinced?" "We can justify our every deed but God looks at our motives" (Proverbs 16:2; 21:2 – TLB).

The renewal of our minds will result in our beginning to think as the Lord thinks and to view situations and people as he views them. Paul's mind was so renewed that he could dare to say that he had the mind of Christ and that he no longer looked at people from a merely human point of view (1 Corinthians 2:16; 2 Corinthians 5:16). His prayer for the Colossian believers was that they too might be thus transformed: "We are asking God that you may see things, as it were, from his point of view by being given spiritual insight and understanding" (Colossians 1:9 – Phillips).

Such a transformation of our minds will enable us to know what pleases God and what does not please him, and thus we shall be able to discern his will easily in the different situations we face. God's promise to us in this New Testament age is, "This is the new agreement (testament) . . . I will write my laws in their minds so that they will know what I want them to do without my even telling them . . . I will write my laws into their minds so that they will always know my will" (Hebrews 8:10; 10:16 – TLB). Such a renewal will give us an understanding not only of God's will, but also of his method and of his purpose. We will know, not only *what* God wants us to do, but also *how* he wants us to do it, and *why*. Doing the will of God can be drudgery if we do not appreciate God's purposes. When we do appreciate them, the will of God becomes for us what it was to Jesus – a delight. It is because of our ignorance of God's nature that we fear his will. If we knew him better, we would rejoice to do his every bidding.

How can our minds be renewed? A wife living close to her husband in heart-companionship comes to know more and more of his mind and of his ways as the years go by. The same applies to the believer and his God. The new birth is like a marriage with the Lord Jesus. We should go on from that point to walk in close fellowship with the Lord, conversing with him day by day.

We must also let him speak to our hearts daily, through his Word as well as through the discipline of trials that he sends into our lives. Thus we shall find ourselves increasingly conformed to the image of our Lord (2 Corinthians 3:18). If we neglect daily meditation on God's Word and prayer fellowship with the Lord, we will find it extremely difficult to ascertain God's mind. Meditation on God's Word can straighten our warped and crooked ways of thinking and make us spiritually minded and sensitive to God's voice.

We can recognize the Lord's voice only by becoming accustomed to hearing it. A new convert once asked a mature servant of God why it was that though Christ had said, "My sheep know my voice," yet he could not hear the Lord's voice. The servant of God replied, "Yes, it is true that his sheep know his voice, but it is also true that the lambs have to learn it."

A son identifies his father's voice easily because he has heard it so often. Even so, it is only by constantly listening to the voice of the Lord that we will be able to distinguish it above the din and clamor of other voices that will ring in our minds when we seek God's will. If you are habituated to listening to the Lord's voice, then in times of emergency, his promise is, "Your ears shall hear a word behind you, saying, This is the way, walk in it, when you turn to the right hand and when you turn to the left" (Isaiah 30:21).

If, on the other hand, we turn to the Lord *only* in times of emergency, we are not likely to hear his voice at all. Some of God's children are so busy that they have no time to listen to the Lord in their daily lives and yet in times of crisis they want to know his will immediately. Speaking of such believers, G. Christian Weiss has said that the spirit of their prayers in an emergency is something like this — "Lord Jesus, I've been awfully busy and haven't had much time to talk with you. Forgive me. But now, Lord, I'm in a predicament, and I must know Your will in this very important matter by 10 o'clock tomorrow morning. So please, Lord, hurry up and reveal it to me. Amen." God's will is not revealed in that way, nor indeed to such persons.

Daily fellowship with God in meditation and in prayer is vital if we wish to have God's guidance in our lives.

SUMMARY

If we want to find God's will, we must first fulfill the following conditions:

1. We must believe that God *will* reveal his will to us. Such faith will be characterized by earnest desire and patience. We should be willing to wait for God's time.
2. We must distrust our own cleverness and humbly lean upon God. We do not have to discard our intellectual abilities, but our confidence must be in God and not in ourselves.
3. We must be willing to do God's will in *every* area of our lives, and not just in a few. We must be obedient to the light God has already given us, and should keep our consciences clean always.
4. We must yield ourselves without reserve to God and be willing to accept *anything* he chooses for us.
5. We must walk with God daily, listening to what he has to say. We must allow him thus to renew our minds and deliver us from worldly thought processes.

CHAPTER THREE

GUIDANCE THROUGH THE INNER WITNESS

When we come to the subject of the means by which God guides us, we must bear in mind that biblical principles are more important than the experiences of even godly men and women. God is not limited to work in any pattern we lay down. He is sovereign and may at times choose to use the miraculous instead of the normal means of guidance. He guided Israel in the wilderness by a pillar of cloud and a pillar of fire, but that method ceased when they entered Canaan.

The Acts of the Apostles have a few cases of extraordinary guidance. An angel spoke to Philip and told him to leave Samaria and to go to the desert road (8:26). Ananias was told by the Lord in a vision to go and meet Saul (9:10-16). Peter saw a vision in which God revealed that he was to take the gospel to the heathen (10: 9-16). Paul saw a vision directing him to go to Macedonia (16:9). He also refers to a time when the Lord gave him directions in a vision in Jerusalem (22:17-21). But these are exceptions rather than the rule.

We cannot entirely dismiss the possibility of God directing his children in similar ways today. But as in the Acts of the Apostles, such instances are rare. In this book we are concerned only with the normal means of guidance.

In the Old Testament, ascertaining God's will appears to have been an easy task. The law of Moses was clear and specific in many things. The Israelites in the wilderness had only to observe and follow the pillar of cloud by day and the pillar of fire by night. They did not have to be spiritual to know when and where to move. They only needed good eyesight! When the high priest sought to find God's will, all he had to do was to cast the "Urim and Thummim" in the Lord's presence and they indicated "Yes" or "No." It was all so simple, because it was external and easily apprehended by man's physical senses.

RELYING ON THE HOLY SPIRIT

In contrast to all this, knowing God's will appears to be so much more difficult for us in this day and age. The reason is that God wants us to *prove* for ourselves what his perfect will is (Romans 12:2). The Holy Spirit now lives in a believer to be his Guide, and he replaces all the external means of guidance that existed in the Old Testament. External guidance is for the immature. Inward guidance is for the mature — and this is the way God desires to lead all his children today.

When seeking God's will, we need to ascertain what the Holy Spirit is saying to us in our spirits. It is essential therefore that we seek to be filled with the Holy Spirit. The Bible says, "Do not be vague *and* thoughtless *and* foolish, but understanding *and* firmly grasping what the will of the Lord is. . . . [therefore] ever be filled . . . with the (Holy) Spirit" (Ephesians 5:17, 18). The words in Luke 4:1 are also significant: "Then Jesus, full of . . . the Holy Spirit . . . was led by the (Holy) Spirit." Throughout his earthly life the Lord Jesus was governed and guided only by the inner witness of the Holy Spirit — never by human coercion or advice or even by sympathetic appeal.

This sensitivity to the voice of the Spirit was found among the early Christians too. In the Acts of the Apostles we find Philip acting on the inner urging of the Spirit and joining the chariot of the Ethiopian statesman (Acts 8:29); Peter obeying the inner voice of the Spirit directing him to go to Cornelius' house (Acts 10:19, 20); and the leaders in the church at Antioch recognizing the witness of the Holy Spirit in their spirits confirming the call of Saul and Barnabas to foreign missionary service (Acts 13:2). The same Spirit desires to guide each of us today in every decision.

RECOGNIZING THE VOICE OF THE SPIRIT

The Holy Spirit speaks to us through an inner pressure on our spirits rather than through an audible voice. He urges us *inwardly* either to take or not to take a certain course of action. Normally, this is the result of much time spent in prayer, weighing the advantages and disadvantages of the proposed course of action. However, the Holy Spirit may also give us a sudden urge at times to go somewhere or to do something. But sudden impulses to do something ridiculous can come from the devil too — or from ourselves. So we must be careful. *The Holy Spirit will in any case never lead us contrary to the teaching of the Bible.*

We can distinguish the voice of the Holy Spirit by the increasing pressure he produces in our spirits and the growing peace he gives to our minds, as we pray over the matter. "The mind set on the Spirit is life and peace" (Romans 8:6 — NASB). The devil's voice is usually harassing and often accompanied by threats of judgment if we do not obey instantly. God invariably gives us sufficient time to consider and be sure of his will.

On some occasions the Spirit may lead us to do something our minds cannot fully understand. Stephen Grellet, an American preacher, was once led by the Spirit to a certain logging camp which he found deserted. But he was so sure of his guidance that he went into the empty dining hall and preached his sermon. Many years later, a man approached Grellet in London. Reminding him of the incident, he said he had been the cook at that camp and had been the only man there that day. He had hidden outside a window and listened to Grellet's sermon. He was converted and had gone on to work for the Lord. Such guidance however is extremely rare.

It is often not easy for us to distinguish between our own heart's voice and the voice of the Spirit, for our hearts are so deceitful. For instance, when considering a possible life partner, we can easily mistake the emotional pressure and the growing feelings of peace and joy at every contemplation of the proposed step, for the witness of the Holy Spirit. The chances of being deceived are, however, considerably lessened, if we examine our motives and make sure we desire the glory of God alone and are prepared to accept whatever *he* chooses for us. It is usually where such yieldedness is lacking or where motives are selfish that we go astray.

God's will may sometimes be just what we like ourselves, but it can also be what we do not instinctively like. We should not think God's will is always the most difficult course of action that lies before us. Neither need it be the easiest course of action. When we are in a difficult situation or a tough job, we may be tempted to run away from the place. This can easily be mistaken for the leading of the Spirit. On such occasions, if we are in doubt, it is better to take the more difficult step and to trust God to give us grace to manifest Christ's victory in our situation.

One practical step when you have to decide on a course of action, would be to draw up a "balance sheet." Draw a line across a sheet of paper and write down on one side all the reasons *for* doing a particular thing and all the reasons *against* it on the other. Pray over these reasons daily and revise the list as necessary. Be sincerely willing to accept either course of action. As you continue to pray, the Holy Spirit will give you a witness in your spirit as to what you are to do.

REALIZING THE IMPORTANCE OF THE SPIRIT

It is essential that we recognize the importance of the inner witness of the Holy Spirit, for this is the chief means by which God guides his children today. We must always obey the inner promptings as well as the inner checks of the Spirit. It is not enough for a Christian to be guided by the principle of right and wrong. That is the plane of the Old Covenant. We are called under God's New Covenant to live on a higher plane — sharing the very life of God and being governed by that life. These two planes of living are symbolized by the two trees in the garden of Eden, the tree of knowledge of good and evil and the tree of life. It is good to have a moral code that tells us what is good and what is evil, and to live by that standard. But that is reverting to living "under the law." The Christian standard is higher (Matthew 5:17-48).

Watchman Nee in his booklet, *Two Principles of Conduct,* says, "It is a most amazing thing that the objective of so many Christians is only conformity to an external standard, though what God has given us by new birth is not a lot of new rules and regulations to which we are required to conform. He has not brought us to a new Sinai and given us a new set of commandments with their 'Thou shalt' and 'Thou shalt not.' . . . As a Christian you now possess the life of Christ, and it is the reactions of His life that you have to consider. If, when you contemplate any move, there is a rise of life within you to make that move; if there is a positive response from the inner life; if there is 'the anointing' within (1 John 2:20, 27); then you can confidently pursue the proposed course. The inner life has indicated that. But if, when you contemplate a certain move, the inner life begins to languish, then you may know that the move you contemplated should be avoided, however commendable it may seem to be.

"Do realize that the conduct of many a *non-Christian* is governed by the principle of right and wrong. Wherein does the Christian differ from the non-Christian if the same principle governs both? God's Word shows us plainly that the Christian is controlled by the life of Christ, not by any external code of ethics. There is something vital within the Christian that responds to what is of God and reacts against what is not of Him; so we must take heed to our inner reactions. . . . We dare not be governed by externalities, nor by reasonings, our own or other people's. Others may approve a certain thing, and when we weigh up the pros and cons we too may think it right; but what is the inner life saying about it?

"Once you realize that the determining factor in all Christian conduct is life, then you know that you must *not only avoid all that is evil, but also all that is just externally good.* Only what issues from the Christian *life* is Christian conduct; therefore we cannot consent to any action that does not spring from life. . . . Many things are right according to human standards, but the Divine standard pronounces them wrong because they lack the Divine life. . . . God's way for us is not known by external indications but by internal registrations. It is peace and joy in the spirit that indicate the Christian's path. It is a fact that the Lord Jesus Christ dwells within the believer, and He is constantly expressing Himself in us, so we must become sensitive to His life and learn to discern what that life is saying."

May God help us to learn this lesson.

SUMMARY

1. God rarely guides us in spectacular ways. In this New Testament age, God guides us through the Holy Spirit. So we must seek to be filled with the Holy Spirit.
2. The Holy Spirit speaks to us through an inner pressure on our spirits. This pressure increases as we wait on God in prayer.
3. To distinguish the voice of the Spirit from other voices, we should examine our motives and see that they are pure.
4. A "balance sheet," to evaluate the advantages and disadvantages of a proposed course of action, can be helpful in enabling us to find God's will.
5. We must place great value on the inner witness of the Holy Spirit, for this is God's chief means of guidance in our day. God expects us to be governed by this in our daily lives and not merely by a moral code.

CHAPTER FOUR

GUIDANCE THROUGH EXTERNAL MEANS

The Holy Spirit speaks to our spirits through the following external means also, when we are seeking his guidance:
1. The teaching of the Bible
2. The witness of circumstances
3. The advice of other believers

If we have ascertained the will of God accurately, the witness of the Holy Spirit through these external means will correspond with his inner witness within our spirits.

THE TEACHING OF THE BIBLE

The Bible has been given that we might be instructed in correct doctrine and be led in the path of righteousness (2 Timothy 3:16, 17). In a number of matters, God's will is already clearly revealed therein.

For example, if you are considering marriage

with an unbeliever (even a nominal Christian and a regular church-goer), the Word of God is explicit: "Do not be unequally yoked up [a symbol of marriage] with unbelievers — do not make mismated alliances with them" (2 Corinthians 6:14).

Similarly, if we see a brother in material need, the Bible clearly teaches that we are to help him (James 2:15, 16; 1 John 3:17). Or if you have a dispute with a fellow-believer and you want to know whether to go to court or not, the Bible emphatically says, "No" (1 Corinthians 6:1-8). The Bible also teaches that lying and theft are always wrong (Ephesians 4:25, 28). If there has been some estrangement between you and another believer, again the Bible leaves no room for doubt as to what you should do. You are to go and be reconciled, taking the initiative yourself, even when it is the other person's fault (Matthew 5:23, 24).

If we have signed a contract or a bond with any firm or institution, there is no need to seek God's will on whether we can break the contract or "jump" the bond, when a more attractive vacancy offers itself elsewhere. The Bible tells us that the person who dwells with God "keeps a promise even if it ruins him" (Psalm 15:4 — TLB), and also that "God delights in those who keep their promises, and abhors those who don't" (Proverbs 12:22 — TLB). It is a shame and a disgrace when a believer does not keep his word.

Besides specific commands, the Word of God

lays down guiding principles too. For example, regarding the acquisition of wealth by games of chance, Proverbs 28:22 (TLB) says, "Trying to get rich quick is evil and leads to poverty" (cf. Proverbs 13:11; 28:20; 1 Timothy 6:9-11). From these passages it is clear that God does not approve of a believer taking part in any form of lottery or betting or gambling.

God's Word is indeed "a flashlight to light the path ahead (of us) and keep (us) from stumbling" (Psalm 119:105 – TLB).

On rare occasions God may *confirm* his guidance to us through some specific passage in our daily Bible reading. But care is needed, for we are often likely to read into a passage what is not basically there. Usually such passages are brought to our attention *without* our looking for them. It is most unwise to look for suggestive verses in our daily Bible reading, for that is not the purpose of the quiet time, and we can easily be led astray thereby. I once heard of a young man who was madly in love with a girl named Patience. Seeking scriptural justification for his desire to marry her, he happened upon a verse which read, "Ye have need of patience." This, to him, was clear evidence that God was encouraging him to go ahead! Our hearts are deceitful and the devil is a subtle foe. We need to be on our guard against both.

God may in his supernatural wisdom lead us through a verse taken out of context, but this is the exception rather than the rule. And when

God employs such a method it will usually be only to confirm guidance that we receive through the normal channels. We should never make such verses the sole basis for guidance in any matter.

THE WITNESS OF CIRCUMSTANCES

God is the God of providence. He can control our circumstances and thereby indicate his will. He allows certain things to befall us either to confirm the guidance we have received through the witness of the Spirit or to stop us from taking a wrong step. As George Mueller has said, "The *stops* of a good man, as well as his *steps* are ordered by the Lord" (cf. Psalm 37:23).

It must be borne in mind though, that Satan too can order circumstances to some extent, to lead us astray. Many have been deceived in choosing a life partner through being guided by circumstances ordered of the devil to trap them! The way to escape deception is by fulfilling the conditions for guidance, mentioned in chapter two.

Circumstances ordered of God must be submitted to and accepted, whereas those arranged by Satan must be resisted. If we are not sure, we can pray something like this, "Lord, I do not know whether this situation is from you or from Satan. But I do want your perfect will at any cost. Save me from being deceived and thus missing your best. If this is from you, I accept it joyfully. If it is from Satan, I resist him and bind him in your Name." The Lord will preserve our way and make all things work together for our good if we are sincere before him *and live according to his commandments* (Proverbs 2:8; Romans 8:28). Satan hindered Paul from going to Thessalonica, but Timothy went instead and God's purposes were still fulfilled (1 Thessalonians 2:18; 3:1, 2).

We find a number of cases of circumstantial guidance in the Acts of the Apostles. God used persecution to scatter the church from Jerusalem for the spread of the gospel (Acts 8:1). Paul and Barnabas moved from one place to another whenever persecution increased to such an extent that there was no point in staying (Acts 13: 50, 51; 14:5, 6, 19, 20). This was in accordance with the Lord's own precept and example (Matthew 10:23; John 7:1). God used a famine to take Saul and Barnabas to Jerusalem (Acts 11: 28-30), where they learned the power of importunate prayer (Acts 12:5). Coming back to Antioch, they imparted this spirit of prayer to their fellow-workers and this finally resulted in the extension of the work to distant regions (Acts 12:25—13:3).

Adverse circumstances in Philippi were used of God to lead Paul and Silas to preach the gospel to a needy jailor (Acts 16:19-34). The last eight chapters of Acts reveal how God used circumstances to lead Paul to preach the gospel to a number of people whom he would not normally have met (cf. Philippians 1:12).

Some of the world's greatest missionaries were guided to their fields by circumstances. David Livingstone initially felt led to go to China and took medical training in preparation for service in that land. When he was ready to go, China was "closed" because of the opium war. The London Missionary Society suggested the West Indies. He turned it down on the grounds that there were many doctors there already. Finally, through contact with pioneer missionary Robert Moffat, Livingstone went to Africa.

Adoniram Judson felt challenged to serve as a missionary in India and accordingly set sail from America. On arrival in India he was not permitted to stay. While in Madras, he was told to leave the country by a certain date. He was therefore compelled to board the only boat leaving Madras before that date. The boat was bound for Burma and Judson spent the rest of his life there.

The work that these two men accomplished for God in these lands clearly proves that it was God who had ordered the circumstances that led them there.

God may prevent us from going into paths he has not chosen for us by putting us on a sick bed or by making us miss a train, an appointment, or an interview. Disappointments can be his appointments for us, if we live under his Lordship. When we do not obtain something we greatly longed for and prayed for, we can be sure that God has something better in store for us.

Missing a train and the delayed arrival of a boat, once led me to speak to a needy soul who opened his heart to the Lord that very night. Transfer to a ship that I did not like was once God's means of leading me to a young Hindu sailor who gave his life to the Lord and was baptized. God makes no mistakes. He is the God of providence. We can trust him to order circumstances for his glory and for our good.

We can ask God at times to reveal his will by altering circumstances, when we find an obstacle in our path. When the Lord called me to resign my commission as an officer in the Indian Navy, I applied for resignation and the application was promptly rejected by the Naval Headquarters. Circumstances were thus contrary to what I felt to be the witness of the Holy Spirit within me. I prayed that the Lord would alter circumstances and release me from the Navy and make that a confirmation of his call. I applied three times for permission to resign my commission. Finally after two years I was released. It was then evident to me that the initial hindrance had been engineered by Satan. Yet God overruled it to strengthen my faith in his total authority over governments and earthly powers and to teach me more of his ways.

Indeed, he is the one who has the key to every door. When he opens a door, no one can shut it, and when he shuts a door, no one can open it (Revelation 3:7). Even a king's heart can be turned by our God in any direction he chooses (Proverbs 21:1; cf. Ezra 6:22).

God may also lead us contrary to circumstances. When the first wave of persecution swept Jerusalem, the apostles did not run away but prayed for boldness. God filled them with his Spirit and made Jerusalem tremble at the manifestation of his power, for his time had not yet come for the disciples to be scattered (Acts 4:29-33; 5:11-14).

When Philip left Samaria for the desert road, it was contrary to circumstances, which called for him to remain in Samaria where he was being greatly used (Acts 8:26).

Circumstances are thus not always an indication of God's will. They must be considered only in conjunction with, and in subjection to the inner witness of the Holy Spirit within our spirits, and his witness through the Bible. God does not expect his children to be pawns moved around by circumstances. He is the Lord of circumstances and he wants his children to share in his mastery over them.

Is it right to ask God to indicate his will by a sign? The Old Testament records some instances of men asking God for a sign to indicate his will. Abraham's servant asked for a sign and thus found the bride God had chosen for Isaac (Genesis 24:10-27). Gideon asked God to confirm his will by a sign. The next night he asked God to reverse the sign. God answered on both occasions and confirmed his will (Judges 6:36-40). The sailors on the ship carrying Jonah drew lots to find who was the cause of the storm. God answered (Jonah 1:7). The casting of lots was used on other occasions as well (Joshua 7:14; 1 Samuel 10:20; 14:41-44; cf. Proverbs 16:33).

In the New Testament there is only one instance of men asking God for a sign to indicate his will, and that too was before the day of Pentecost (Acts 1:23-26). Note that after the advent of the Holy Spirit, there is not a single recorded case in the New Testament of believers seeking to find God's will through a sign. This seems to indicate that it is no longer God's normal method of guidance. It served a purpose in Old Testament times when the Holy Spirit did not indwell man — but not now.

God may *confirm* his will or encourage our fainting spirits with an occasional sign. When other methods of guidance are apparently inconclusive, only then dare we ask God for a sign. But we should pray even about the type of sign to ask for. We should not use signs as a means of getting our own way. For instance, we should not ask God for a miracle as a sign, when our real intention is to get some excuse for not going along the path we know he wants us to take. At the same time, we shouldn't ask God for something so common that it is not really a sign at all, just as an excuse for going along our own self-chosen path.

We should also beware of the procedure adopted by some Christians who ask God for a verse as a sign and then shut their eyes, open their Bibles and place their finger on the page that falls open. That method can lead us astray and in any case is foolish. The Bible is not a book of magic! Don't treat it as if it were.

To make a sign the chief, or the only means of guidance is totally unscriptural. We should remember too that desiring signs is a mark of spiritual immaturity. We should grow out of that state as soon as possible.

THE ADVICE OF OTHER BELIEVERS

The New Testament places great emphasis on the necessity of believers functioning together as members of one body. No member can function independently; everyone is dependent on others for existence and survival. It is quite reasonable therefore to expect that even in guidance God would place great value on the fellowship of believers. He has made this provision as a safeguard against our missing his perfect will.

By ourselves we may not be able to see all the advantages and disadvantages of taking a certain step. The advice of other godly men will be invaluable in helping us to look from different angles at the decision we are taking. This is especially necessary when facing a major decision. If, in proud self-sufficiency, we ignore this God-ordained means of guidance, we will suffer loss. The Bible says, "There is safety in many counselors. . . . Don't go ahead with your plans without the advice of others. . . . The advice of a wise man refreshes like water from a mountain spring. Those accepting it become aware of the pitfalls on ahead. . . . A fool thinks he needs no advice, but a wise man listens to others. . . . The good man asks advice from friends; the wicked plunge ahead — and fall" (Proverbs 24:6; 20:18; 13:14; 12:15, 26 — TLB).

However, there are two extremes to avoid. One is to be completely independent of the advice of godly men. The other is to be so completely dependent on their advice as to accept it without question as God's perfect will. If we cling to either of these extremes, we shall either go astray or remain spiritually stunted all our lives. Much as God wants us to take counsel from our fellow-believers, he does not expect us to be slavishly subject to their advice — even if they are saintly men.

The Bible presents truth in a perfect balance. Man, unfortunately, has a tendency to swing to an extreme. It is thus that many heresies have been born in Christendom.

In the Old Testament, this balanced view is clearly presented in 1 Kings, chapters 12 and 13. In chapter 12, the young king Rehoboam should have taken the advice of the godly elders instead of listening to young men like himself. Because he didn't, he precipitated the division of his kingdom. In chapter 13, the young prophet should *not* have listened to the advice of the older prophet (cf. Job 32:9). Because he did, he lost his life.

In the New Testament, we see this balance in the life of the Apostle Paul. In Acts 13:1-3, we find God calling Paul for foreign missionary service. But God revealed his will for Paul to his fellow-workers also at the same time. What God spoke to Paul privately was thus confirmed to him through the others. On the other hand, in Acts 21:1-15, we find Paul rejecting the advice of every one of his fellow-believers (and even the prophecies of some of them) and going in the direction *he* felt was God's will for him. God later confirmed that his going to Jerusalem was right (Acts 23:11).

On yet another occasion, at the beginning of Paul's Christian life, he went to Arabia, having found the will of God entirely on his own without consulting anyone at all (Galatians 1:15-17).

These examples from God's Word suggest that there are some occasions when we should pay attention to the advice of godly men, some occasions when we may have to go against the advice of those same men, and yet other occasions when we do not have to consult anyone at all. In any case, whether we accept or reject or do not seek the advice of others, *the ultimate decision must always be our own,* for we are personally answerable to God for our decisions. The advice of a man of God can be invaluable but is never infallible.

Michael Harper in his book *Prophecy — A Gift for the Body of Christ* writes: "Prophecies which tell other people what they are to do, are to be regarded with great suspicion. 'Guidance' is never indicated as one of the uses of prophecy. Paul was told what would happen to him if he went to Jerusalem, but not told either to go or refrain from going. His friends may have advised him concerning this, but the guidance did not come from the prophecy. Agabus foretold a famine, but his prophecy gave no instructions as to what should be done about it. On the whole in the New Testament guidance is given direct to the individual, not through another person, as was common in the Old Testament. For instance, although Cornelius was told by an angel to send for Peter (Acts 10:5), Peter himself was told to go with them through an independent agency, (Acts 10:20)."

In his booklet *Guidance*, James McConkey writes, "Flesh and blood could not reveal the Christ to Simon Peter (Matthew 16:17). Neither can it reveal the things of Christ to us. Nor does it matter whether it is our own flesh and blood or that of some other. For the other man's flesh and blood is compassed with the same infirmities and subject to the same errors as ours. Moreover the man who relies upon his friends for his guidance soon finds that the variety of advice they offer only increases the number of his perplexities. Then too it is a Divine principle that God does not reveal to another man His plans for your life. Christ's rebuke of Peter for wanting to know His will for John is the clearest possible proof of this (John 21:22). You may help the little child to walk in its beginnings of the art. But if it is ever to learn to walk alone there comes a time when it must let go of your hand entirely and cease from all dependence upon you. The believer who would learn to walk with God must learn the same lesson. And as a baby learns it at the cost of some tumbles even so must the Christian learn it at the cost of some mistakes. It were better learned that way than not to be learned at all. The price of a few blunders is not too high for such a treasure as a walk alone with God in the place of His own God-given guidance. Does God then have no place for your Christian friends in this matter of guidance? He surely does. Get all the help; all the light upon God's Word; all the experience of others you possibly can. That is, you may get the *facts* from others. But you must make your *decisions* yourself. For when we reach the place of decision we cannot evade the personal, patient waiting upon God alone, through which we learn the most precious lessons of His guidance."

Nevertheless, whenever we do have to go against the advice of mature believers, let us check our own guidance repeatedly to make sure it is indeed God who is leading us. This must especially be remembered when making major decisions.

THE VOICE OF THE LORD

On the mount of transfiguration, Peter was rebuked by God for attempting to place the Lord Jesus on the same level as Moses and Elijah. These men were indeed God's spokesmen in Old Testament times, but a new age was dawning and Peter had to recognize that. In this new age there was to be only one Spokesman — "This is My Son, . . . the Beloved One; be constantly listening to and obeying Him" (Mark 9:7). And so when the disciples looked up again, "they suddenly no longer saw anyone with them except *Jesus only.*" It is the voice of the Lord that we must ultimately hear, whatever external means God may use to speak to us.

In *What Shall This Man Do?* Watchman Nee says, "Christianity always involves a personal knowledge of God through His Spirit, and not *merely* the knowing of His will through the medium of a man or a book. . . . Thus in practical terms today, we have the written Scriptures, represented by Moses, and we have the living human messenger, represented by Elijah who never tasted death. These two God-given gifts to every believer are among the most precious factors that contribute to our Christian life: the Book of God in our hand to instruct us, and the friend who lives close to the Lord and who can often make known to us what the Lord has shown him. The Book is always right; the counsel of a friend so often is. We need God's Book and we need God's prophets. He would not have us discard either. But the lesson of this incident on the mount of transfiguration is surely that neither of these can take the place of the living voice of God to our hearts.

"We dare not despise God's messengers. We need again and again the arresting challenge of a truly prophetic spoken word or the calm of mature spiritual instruction. But we do not commit ourselves totally and exclusively to the revelation which comes through holy men of God, however sound it be. We are under duty bound to listen to the voice of the Lord and to follow Him.

"Still less dare we despise God's written Word. The inspired Scriptures of truth are vital to our life and progress, and we would not — we dare not — be without them. Nevertheless there are those of us who may be in danger of looking to the letter of the Word even more than to Jesus Christ Himself as our final authority. What the Bible says we set ourselves to carry out, religiously and in detail, and God may honour us for that. Yet if, in doing so, we go further, and exalt the Bible to a position where our use of it challenges even the very Lordship of Christ Himself, we may run the risk of remaining tragically out of touch with *Him*. . . .

"(Christianity) demands a personal, first-hand intelligence of the will of God, that embraces these other God-given aids but that does not end with them."

The secret of guidance lies in hearing the voice of the Lord.

SUMMARY

1. The Holy Spirit guides us through the teaching of the Bible when we are seeking his guidance.
   (a) In many areas the Bible has already revealed what God's will is.
   (b) God may confirm his guidance through a passage in our daily Bible reading. But this should never be made the sole basis for guidance in any matter.
2. The Holy Spirit often speaks to us through the witness of circumstances.
   (a) God can use circumstances either to confirm the guidance we have received or to prevent our taking a wrong step.
   (b) But Satan too can order our circumstances to some extent. So they are not always an indication of God's will.
   (c) God may lead us at times contrary to circumstances. We can also ask God to reveal his will by altering circumstances.
   (d) God may occasionally confirm his guidance to us by means of a sign. However, asking for signs is a mark of spiritual immaturity and we should grow out of that state as soon as possible.
3. The Holy Spirit may speak to us through the advice of other believers.

(a) God has made this provision as a safeguard against our missing his will.
(b) The advice of godly men will enable us to see other aspects of a particular matter which we may have failed to consider.
(c) There are some occasions when we should pay attention to the advice of godly men, some occasions when we may have to go against the advice of those same men, and yet other occasions when we do not have to consult anyone at all.
(d) We should never be governed by the advice of other believers alone. The final decision must *always be our own*. But when we have to go against the advice of godly men, we should check and recheck our guidance.
4. Whatever means God may use, the supremely important thing is to hear *his* voice.

CHAPTER FIVE

VOCATIONAL CALLING

One of the first major problems of guidance faced by young people is knowing what vocation God wants them to take up and where they should work.

God's perfect will in vocation needs to be sought not only by those contemplating professional Christian service, but by every believer. As mentioned in chapter one, God has planned a vocation for each of his children. It is essential then that we seek to find out what it is. If God's calling for you is to be a teacher in a school, you would be disobedient if you became a pastor. It would be foolish to go as a missionary to a foreign land if God wanted you to stay at home. Likewise, don't waste your life as a businessman at home if God wants you to be a pioneer evangelist among those who have never heard the Good News.

THE VOCATION OF GOD'S CHOICE

Nevertheless, every believer should be a full-time witness of the Lord Jesus Christ even if he is not in full-time Christian service. A Christian doctor when asked his profession replied, "My profession is to be a witness for the Lord Jesus Christ and to bring souls to him. I work as a doctor to pay the expenses." Indeed, he had the right perspective.

When vocation is considered from this viewpoint, we need not fear the possibility of missing God's will. It is when personal advancement and prestige influence our choice that we go astray.

How should a young believer go about the matter of finding God's will in this realm? Where the option of choosing a career is still open before him, he should consider his intellectual aptitude and study for the vocation most fitting to him. He should select a vocation only after much prayer. In the absence of any check in his spirit after prayer, he should go ahead and consider the vocation he is most suited for. He should never, in any case, allow himself to be pushed into a vocation selected for him by someone else.

Those who are already in college may be limited in their selection of a vocation. Such need not fear that they might have missed God's will. God is sovereign and overrules in our lives when we are ignorant of his ways. He lays his hand upon us and steers our course, unknown to us, long before we come to a place of surrender to him. He holds us responsible only after he speaks to us.

THE PLACE OF GOD'S CHOICE

Throughout his student days, a believer should be much in prayer that God will give him the right information about job opportunities and contacts with the right people and institutions, so that he will, on completion of his studies, be able to go to the place of God's choice. He should constantly bear in mind the Lord's words in Matthew 9:37: "The harvest is indeed plentiful, but the laborers are few." In obedience to the Lord's command in John 4:35, he should seek to get details of the Lord's work in various parts of his country and of the world. He should be ready to go wherever the Lord may have need of him — whether as a teacher, a nurse, an engineer, or whatever his vocation may be. It is a shame that so many seek personal comfort and have no concern for the spread of the gospel and for the salvation of souls.

He must then seek the advice and prayer fellowship of mature believers (in his own locality or elsewhere), who are interested in him and who are aware of the situation in the areas where he is seeking employment. He should also try to understand what God is saying to him through his circumstances. With all this information in hand, when the time draws near to make a decision, he should seek to ascertain what the Holy Spirit is saying within his own spirit. He should finally base his decision on this witness of the Spirit within him, trusting God even then to turn him around in case he has been mistaken.

THE CHRISTIAN MINISTRY AND MISSIONARY SERVICE

A few words need to be said here about the Christian ministry and foreign missionary service. God calls only a small percentage of believers into such a ministry, even as he called only one tribe in twelve in Israel to the service of the temple. But he expects all his children to be willing, should he call them. Every believer should therefore consider these callings and seek with all his heart to know whether or not God wants him in them.

One who stays in his homeland or works in a secular vocation should be equally sure that God wants him there. The calling to be an evangelist is not a more spiritual one than the calling to be an engineer or an accountant. It is not more spiritual to serve God abroad than in your homeland. The important thing is to be *what* God wants you to be, and to be *where* he wants you to be. He requires obedience before sacrifice (1 Samuel 15:22).

A decision to enter full-time Christian service

should be taken coolly, not in the emotionally tense atmosphere of a meeting nor under pressure from any man. Hasty decisions are usually regretted later on. God always gives us ample time to be sure of his will before we decide.

The call to an exclusively Christian ministry is not easily defined. As with all other guidance, it comes in different forms to different people. In some rare cases, it may come in a vision or through an audible voice. Esther Butler, pioneer missionary in China in the early part of this century, said when God called her to this work she saw a crowded Chinese street in a vision. She later clearly recognized the faces and places on arrival in Nanking.

To others, the call has come as an inward urge based purely on sanctified logic. John G. Paton went from Scotland to the South Pacific islands as a missionary because he felt the people there had less opportunity to hear the message than those in Scotland. James Gilmour went to Mongolia because, he said, he did not receive a call to stay in his home country. Their accomplishments for God in these places clearly show they lived in God's perfect will for their lives.

What form the call takes is unimportant. But the one who goes into a professional Christian ministry cannot afford to be unsure of his call. He cannot recruit himself into this ministry, nor can another recruit him. That prerogative remains forever in the hands of God alone.

In most cases, a person called to the Christian

ministry or missionary service will find God confirming his call through circumstances and through Spirit-filled believers. However there can be, and have been, exceptions to this rule, for God cannot be bound to any fixed pattern. Yet some guidelines can be laid down: God calls those who are active in his work in their secular occupations. He speaks only to those who are seeking to be his witnesses in their present circumstances. He is a rewarder of those who diligently seek him.

We must also remember that the calling of God is not a static thing. God may lead you into exclusively Christian work for a time and then lead you to be his witness in a secular occupation. He may take you to a distant land as a missionary for some years and then bring you back to work for him in your homeland — or vice versa. We must be willing to move with God as situations and circumstances change, and not remain in bondage to tradition and the opinions of men.

Whether we are in a secular job or in exclusively Christian work, whether in the homeland or abroad, our calling is equally to be a servant of God. The nature and sphere of work may differ, but we are all called to represent the Lord worthily before others and to bring them to a saving knowledge of him. God has a specific place in his vast vineyard for you. As the hymn says, "There's a work for Jesus none but you can do." It is your responsibility to find out what that is and to make sure you fulfill it.

"God ordained you to your work — see that you don't fail him" (Colossians 4:17 — Phillips).

SUMMARY

1. God has a specific vocation for you. Your duty is to fulfill that.
2. Every believer, irrespective of his vocation, is called to be a full-time witness of the Lord Jesus.
3. A young person seeking God's guidance about his vocation should prepare himself for that for which he is most suited, in the absence of any indication from God to the contrary.
4. When looking for a job, he should find out information concerning the needs of the Lord's work in different places. He should be much in prayer and, after consulting mature believers and considering his circumstances, he should finally be guided by the inner witness of the Holy Spirit.
5. No person should go into the Christian ministry or into missionary service without a clear call from God.
6. The calling of God is a dynamic thing. We must be willing to move with him into any new sphere of work, when and as he calls.

CHAPTER SIX

FINAL CONSIDERATIONS

It should be evident to the reader by now that no perfect formula exists for infallible guidance. Very often we will be faced with perplexity when seeking to know God's will. God permits this so that we may press closer to him and thus know more of his mind and receive more of his life.

Times of uncertainty are also used by God to sift our motives. When unsure of God's will, we should examine ourselves to see whether we have fulfilled the prerequisites for his guidance (mentioned in chapter two).

God uses perplexity to exercise and strengthen our faith also. "Who among you fears the Lord and obeys his Servant [the Lord Jesus]? If such men walk in darkness, without one ray of light, let them trust the Lord, let them rely upon their God" (Isaiah 50:10 — TLB). We should not therefore be surprised or discouraged when we encounter perplexity. Even the apostle Paul was often perplexed, but he never despaired or gave up (2 Corinthians 4:8). God may sometimes show us his will just before we have to make a decision; he may keep us waiting a long time prior to that.

In any case, he will show us only the next step at each stage. He leads us step by step because he wants us to depend on him day by day, and to walk by faith and not by sight. When he shows us only one step at a time, we are compelled to lean on him. Moreover, if God showed us the whole future, it is quite likely that we would not want to obey him fully. And so he shows us just one step at a time and gradually makes us willing to fulfill all his will. To find God's will, therefore, all we need to do at any time is to take the next step that God shows us. As we do so, we will find God's plan unfolding gradually.

There is an ancient Chinese proverb that says, "A journey of a thousand miles begins with but a single step." Abraham went out from his home country not knowing where he was finally going. He only knew that God was leading him (Hebrews 11:8). He obeyed God at every step and God did not disappoint him. None who follow God as Abraham did need ever fear disappointment.

DELIVERANCE FROM INDECISION

Many times we will have to take a step forward while still not *perfectly* sure about God's will. This too is a part of the discipline of walking by *faith*, for certainty can sometimes be the equivalent of walking by sight. God sometimes gives us clear assurances to encourage us lest we faint. But many times he expects us to move forward *without* visible evidences of his approval. Having ascertained the mind of the Holy Spirit to the best of our knowledge, we should move ahead without waiting indefinitely. The Bible says, "We should make plans — counting on God to direct us" (Proverbs 16:9 — TLB). Looking back over such decisions later, we will find that in spite of the dimness of our vision, God did not let us go astray. In other words, although there may have been much uncertainty in *prospect*, there will be much certainty and rejoicing in *retrospect*.

"The very dimness of my sight
  Makes me secure,
For groping in my misty way
I feel His Hand, I hear Him say,
  'My help is sure.'"

J. Oswald Sanders in *Spiritual Leadership* says: "It might be thought by those who have not found themselves in a position of leadership, that greater experience and a longer walk with God would result in much greater ease in discerning the will of God in perplexing situations.

But the reverse is often the case. God treats the leader as a mature adult, leaving more and more to his spiritual discernment, and giving fewer sensible and tangible evidences of His guidance than in earlier years."

Hudson Taylor, founder of the China Inland Mission, once said in relation to guidance, that in his younger days things used to come to him so clearly and so quickly. "But," he said, "now as I have gone on, and God has used me more and more, I seem often to be like a man going along in a fog. I do not know what to do" (quoted in *D. E. Hoste* by Phyllis Thompson). Yet whenever a decision was made, God always honored Hudson Taylor's trust.

If when taking a step in uncertainty we miss the path of God's perfect will, he can be trusted to divert us. The promise in Isaiah 30:21 (TLB) is, "If you leave God's paths and go astray, you will hear a Voice behind you say, 'No, this is the way; walk here.'" God can order circumstances to alter our course when we miss the road. But we should not remain in perpetual inaction waiting for spectacular guidance for every move. A ship can be turned around much quicker when moving than when stationary; so can we.

In Acts 16:6-10, Paul and Silas tried to go into Asia, not as a result of any clear leading from the Lord but desiring to do his will. They were hindered — perhaps by God-ordered circumstances. Next they attempted to enter Bithynia.

Again their way was blocked. But because they were actively seeking God's will and not passively waiting for guidance, he led them finally to the place of his choice — Macedonia.

In the smaller details of daily life, guidance is not necessarily a question of constant conscious inquiry. It is a matter of walking in the Spirit. Right relationship with the Lord will lead to right action. In such small details, the guidance of God is not something that we need be acutely aware of all the time. We may be unconscious of it. It is our basic relationship with the Lord that is the important factor, for guidance is a spiritual matter and not a mechanical technique.

DELIVERANCE FROM REGRET

Regrets over past failure may torment the minds of some of us. We may have missed God's will in some issue and are now unable to correct it. But regret is futile, for it will only eat up our spiritual vitality and leave us totally unfit for any service for God. Failure should be confessed to God who is faithful to forgive us and to cleanse us immediately (1 John 1:7, 9). He has also promised not to remember our past sins (Hebrews 8:12). If God does not harp on our past there is no need for us to agonize over it. We should therefore turn our back once and for all on those failures. It may not be possible to rectify the blunders, but we can ask the Lord to use the rest of our life for his glory.

David fell very low when he sinned with Bathsheba and then murdered her husband, Uriah. Yet, instead of living the rest of his life in regret, he came back to God in brokenness and repentance. Accepting God's forgiveness, he lived thereafter for God's glory. The Holy Spirit recorded later that David pleased the Lord in all his life, except in the matter of Uriah (1 Kings 15:5). If David had allowed regret to plague his mind, he would only have grieved the Lord further. Those who live with the weight of regret perpetually on their minds only succeed in adding failure to failure. We must forget past failures and press forward to fulfill God's will (cf. Phil. 3:13, 14). God can restore to us the years that have been lost (Joel 2:25).

Another temptation is to worry over a past decision which at the time we felt convinced was in the will of God, but which we now doubt. Perhaps the decision has led us into trouble. Or maybe we are now aware of facts which, had we known then, might have led to a different decision. The principle we should always bear in mind is: never doubt in the darkness what God has shown in the light. If we sincerely sought the will of God and decided according to the light we then had, there is no need to look back now in regret. God is not a cruel despot who delights in making fools of us. He is a loving Father, and he will not give us a stone if we ask for bread. If we sought his will sincerely, we can be sure God overruled everything to let us decide rightly. Even the facts that we were ignorant of then, must have been withheld by God with a purpose.

God gave Paul and Silas clear directions at Troas to go to Macedonia, and they went immediately. Yet soon after arrival, they were locked up in prison with their feet in stocks. They could have wondered then whether their sense of guidance was wrong. Had they known their fate in advance they might never have left Troas. But God gave them no warning. Though put in prison, Paul and Silas trusted God. Refusing to doubt in the darkness what God had shown them in the light, they continued to praise him (Acts 16:8-26). Later events clearly showed they were indeed in the will of God. Getting into trouble is, by itself, no indication that we are out of God's will. If we trust God we shall praise him in the thickest darkness without any regrets.

DELIVERANCE FROM FEAR

Fear of men and of circumstances can make us miss the will of God. Many believers are governed by considerations of security and safety when seeking guidance. They feel that a certain place or occupation is insecure and dangerous, and so rule it out of their minds altogether. But there is no place or occupation in this world totally free from danger. The safest place in all the world is always the center of

God's perfect will. We step into danger only when we step out of God's plan. The one who makes his decisions without seeking God's guidance will be vulnerable to Satan's attacks. But "the one who lives and works in the appointed place of the Most High will be protected by the shadow of the Almighty" (Psalm 91:1 — adapted).

We need to be delivered too, from the fear of making mistakes. The man who never makes a mistake is the man who never does anything. We are students in God's school and we shall doubtless go wrong occasionally. But the Lord is ever near, ready to put things right. Apart from the Lord Jesus himself, no man ever learned to walk in God's perfect will without making many mistakes. The greatest saints learned to walk in the will of God just as a child learns to walk — through many falls. The child who is afraid of falling may never learn to walk! We must never let such fear keep us from moving forward. Walking in God's will may not be easy but it is a great adventure with him and he has promised to hold us when we fall — "The steps of good men are directed by the Lord. . . . If they fall it isn't fatal, for the Lord holds them with his hand" (Psalm 37:23, 24 — TLB).

Finally, remember that guidance is essentially a personal matter between God and you. The way God led another person may not be the way he wishes to lead you. The broad principles are the same for all believers, but the exact mode varies from individual to individual. You will only be confused if you seek for the same type of guidance you heard someone else describe in his testimony. Leave it to God how he should guide you. Let your one concern be that you might always be available to him, to do whatever he desires. He will make it his concern to make you aware of his will and strengthen you to fulfill it.

> "Why do I drift on a storm-tossed sea,
> With neither compass, nor star, nor chart,
> When, as I drift, God's own plan for me,
> Waits at the door of my slow-trusting heart?
>
> Down from the heavens it drops like a scroll;
> Each day a bit will the Master unroll.
> Each day a mite of the veil will He lift;
> Why do I falter? Why wander, and drift?
>
> Drifting, while God's at the helm to steer;
> Groping, when God lays the course, so clear;
> Swerving, though straight into port I might sail;
> Wrecking, when Heaven lies just within hail.
>
> Help me, O God, in the plan to believe:
> Help me my fragment each day to receive,
> Oh, that my will may with Thine have no strife!
> God-yielded wills find the God-planned life."
> — *Selected*

SUMMARY

1. God permits perplexity in order that we may know him better. He also sifts our

motives and strengthens our faith thereby.
2. In most cases, we should move forward even when vague about God's will, provided we have ascertained the mind of the Spirit to the best of our knowledge. We should not wait indefinitely.
3. We should not look back in regret over past failures or past decisions.
4. We must never let either fear of danger or fear of making a mistake keep us in perpetual inaction.
5. We should leave it to God as to *how* he guides us.